ADAPTIVE LEADERSHIP

Decision-Making in a Fast-Paced World

CONSULTORIA IA

Copyright © 2024 CONSULTORIA IA

All rights reserved

The characters and events portrayed in this book are fictitious. Any similarity to real persons, living or dead, is coincidental and not intended by the author.

No part of this book may be reproduced, or stored in a retrieval system, or transmitted in any form or by any means, electronic, mechanical, photocopying, recording, or otherwise, without express written permission of the publisher.

Cover design by: Art Painter
Library of Congress Control Number: 2018675309
Printed in the United States of America

TO OUR FAMILY

CONTENTS

Title Page

Copyright

Dedication

Overview

Why Read This Book?

Target Audience

Prologue

Chapter 1: Embracing the Adaptive Leader's Mindset

Chapter 2: Reading the Terrain: Sensing, Interpreting, and Responding in Real Time

Chapter 3: Mastering Decision-Making in Uncertain Times

Chapter 4: The Adaptive Mindset in Decision-Making

Scene: A quiet café in Palo Alto.

Key Reflections on the Adaptive Mindset in Leadership

2. Balancing Vision with Real-Time Flexibility

3. Embracing Failure as a Growth Mechanism

4. Building a Purpose-Driven Culture

5. The Importance of a North Star Vision

Practical Challenges in Adaptive Leadership

2. Encouraging Experimentation Without Compromising Quality

3. Sustaining Team Alignment Under High Pressure

4. Managing Information Overload and Decision Fatigue

Developing Skills for an Adaptive Mindset

Statistical Overview: Adaptation in Modern Business

Challenges and Reflections for Adaptive Leaders

Chapter 5: Navigating the Controversies and Challenges of Adaptive Leadership

Controversy 1: The Paradox of Flexibility and Stability

Controversy 2: Ethics in Adaptive Leadership

Future Challenge 1: Adapting to AI and Automation

Future Challenge 2: Leading Through Environmental Uncertainty

Controversy 3: The Inclusivity Gap in Adaptive Leadership

Future Challenge 3: Addressing Mental Health in Fast-Paced Environments

The Path Forward for Adaptive Leaders

Overview of Key Adaptive Leadership Challenges: A Data Snapshot

Adaptive Leadership and Technological Disruption

Advice for Leaders:

Sustainability: Balancing Profitability with Environmental Responsibility

Advice for Leaders:

The Inclusivity Imperative in Adaptive Leadership

Advice for Leaders:

Mental Health: Building Resilient, Supportive Workplaces

Advice for Leaders:

The Future Path for Adaptive Leaders: Practical Tips and Takeaways

Appendices

Appendix A: Key Concepts and Terminology in Adaptive Leadership

Appendix B: Practical Frameworks for Adaptive Leadership

Appendix C: Statistics and Data on Adaptive Leadership

Appendix D: Real-World Case Studies in Adaptive Leadership

Appendix E: Further Reading and Resources

Appendix F: Common Challenges in Adaptive Leadership and Solutions

OVERVIEW

Adaptive Leadership: Decision-Making in a Fast-Paced World explores the essential strategies and skills leaders need to excel in today's dynamic environment. With rapid changes and high stakes, traditional leadership models often fall short. This eBook provides a practical guide for making swift, informed decisions, empowering leaders to navigate complexity and uncertainty with confidence. Readers will gain insights into adaptive frameworks, resilience-building techniques, and tools for fostering a flexible, forward-thinking culture. Perfect for executives, managers, and emerging leaders, this book equips readers to thrive in any industry by harnessing the power of adaptability in real-time decision-making.

WHY READ THIS BOOK?

In an era marked by rapid changes, uncertainty, and complex challenges, leaders can no longer rely solely on traditional strategies. *Adaptive Leadership: Decision-Making in a Fast-Paced World* is designed to equip leaders with the mindset, tools, and frameworks needed to thrive in high-stakes environments. This book offers actionable insights on how to make informed, agile decisions, manage uncertainty, and lead with resilience. By reading this book, you'll gain practical techniques for navigating unpredictable situations and fostering a culture of adaptability, preparing you to lead confidently through any challenge. Whether you're an established leader or just starting, this guide is essential for anyone who wants to stay ahead in today's fast-paced world.

TARGET AUDIENCE

This book is ideal for leaders, managers, and professionals across all industries who want to sharpen their decision-making skills in dynamic and high-pressure environments. Whether you're a CEO, mid-level manager, startup founder, or aspiring leader, *Adaptive Leadership* offers practical strategies for those looking to enhance their adaptability and thrive amid rapid change. Additionally, HR professionals, organizational consultants, and educators will find valuable insights to guide others in cultivating a resilient, forward-thinking culture. Perfect for anyone committed to driving growth and innovation in today's fast-paced world, this book is your roadmap to effective, adaptive leadership.

PROLOGUE

In a world that's moving faster than ever before, the demands on leaders have evolved. Traditional approaches, built for a more predictable landscape, often fall short in helping us navigate the uncharted territories of constant change. As industries are reshaped by rapid technological advancements, global interconnectivity, and shifting market dynamics, today's leaders face an urgent need for adaptability.

The goal of this book is not only to highlight the importance of adaptive leadership but to provide a toolkit for mastering it. Adaptive leadership is about embracing uncertainty, making informed decisions under pressure, and cultivating the resilience to pivot when necessary. This isn't just a skill set for survival—it's a foundation for innovation, growth, and impact.

Throughout these pages, you'll encounter real-world examples, proven strategies, and actionable frameworks that will empower you to make better decisions, manage complexity, and inspire those you lead. The chapters ahead are designed to meet you where you are, whether you're a seasoned executive, a manager in a fast-evolving industry, or an entrepreneur looking to scale your vision.

Welcome to *Adaptive Leadership: Decision-Making in a Fast-Paced World.* Here's to the journey of leading with agility, vision, and purpose in a world that waits for no one.

CHAPTER 1: EMBRACING THE ADAPTIVE LEADER'S MINDSET

In the rapidly shifting landscape of our world, leaders are confronted daily with challenges that defy traditional approaches. Organizations once guided by structured hierarchies and stable routines now find themselves in a chaotic environment where yesterday's certainty is today's liability. Amidst the accelerated rhythm of change—spurred by technological advances, global markets, and an increasingly interconnected society—the call for adaptive leadership has never been louder. This chapter invites you to explore the core of what it means to be an adaptive leader, a mindset that transcends management and enters the realm of continual evolution, responsiveness, and proactive resilience.

The Need for Adaptability in a Complex World

Gone are the days when one could assume that a strong leadership strategy would withstand the test of time. The world's interconnectedness has introduced layers of complexity and ambiguity that make traditional problem-solving methods inadequate. Today, a leader must do more than make decisions; they must navigate uncertainty, recognize emerging trends, and respond with agility. To lead adaptively is to understand that change is not a hurdle to overcome but the very environment within which success must be sought.

Consider the dynamic between structured and flexible thinking. Structured thinking served as the bedrock of past leadership, a method that called for a fixed set of rules to dictate organizational behavior. However, in the current climate, an over-reliance on rigidity can prove disastrous. Adaptive leadership demands a shift towards a learning mindset, one that embraces curiosity, values diverse perspectives, and prioritizes continuous learning. This mindset is critical in addressing complex problems where solutions are often neither obvious nor straightforward. Embracing adaptability allows leaders to confront complexity head-on, turning potential roadblocks into opportunities for growth.

In many ways, adaptive leadership embodies a shift from being a problem-solver to being a problem-framer. Leaders who frame problems effectively can empower their teams to explore innovative solutions. A traditional leader might focus on efficiency, asking how to do things right, while an adaptive leader concentrates on doing the right things, even if those things are uncharted or unconventional. This shift in thinking enables organizations to be not only reactive to change but also proactive in anticipating it.

Breaking Free from the "Hero" Leader Mentality

For decades, we've been captivated by the notion of the "hero" leader: the individual with all the answers, the one who steps in to save the day. But in a world that demands responsiveness and agility, this model no longer serves us. Adaptive leadership moves beyond the myth of the lone hero, embracing instead a more collective approach to decision-making. The truth is, no single leader can anticipate every challenge or craft the perfect solution in isolation. By fostering a culture that values input from all levels of an organization, leaders can leverage a broader pool of insights, making decisions that are not only timely but also enriched by a diversity of perspectives.

In the adaptive model, a leader's role shifts from controlling outcomes to facilitating processes. Instead of dictating every step, adaptive leaders empower others to take ownership of their work, building a network of shared accountability. This style of leadership reduces bottlenecks and opens the floor for fresh ideas to emerge from unexpected places within the organization. Moreover, it reflects a commitment to cultivating a culture where employees are encouraged to experiment, even if it means learning from mistakes. Leaders who embrace this approach demonstrate a willingness to be vulnerable, to admit when they don't have all the answers, and to see mistakes as critical components of the learning process.

Transitioning from a hero leader to an adaptive leader requires not only a change in mindset but also a deep commitment to personal development. Self-reflection becomes crucial; leaders must constantly assess their beliefs, values, and assumptions. By cultivating a practice of introspection, adaptive leaders stay aware of their biases, maintain open minds, and respond more authentically to the evolving needs of their organizations.

Balancing Stability and Change

In the world of adaptive leadership, balance is key. Leaders are tasked with the delicate challenge of maintaining organizational stability while simultaneously embracing the inevitability of change. This dual focus can seem paradoxical—how does one provide stability while fostering an environment open to disruption? The answer lies in viewing stability not as resistance to change but as the establishment of core values and a clear purpose that guide the organization through transitions.

When leaders anchor their organizations in a strong sense of purpose, they create a resilient foundation that allows for flexibility. For instance, companies like Apple and Tesla have not only adapted to change but have been drivers of it, transforming entire industries. These organizations are not rigid, yet they possess an unwavering commitment to their core values, which creates a sense of stability even as they disrupt markets. Adaptive leaders understand that purpose provides a constant amidst flux, helping teams navigate uncertainty with a clear direction.

Balancing stability and change also requires leaders to recognize when to pursue incremental improvements and when to leap toward transformative innovation. Incremental changes offer a measure of predictability, giving the organization a steady pace of growth. However, transformative change—often unsettling and disruptive—opens the door to exponential progress. Adaptive leaders are adept at reading the signs, discerning when stability is needed and when bold change is required to move forward. This ability to toggle between incremental and transformative actions is a hallmark of the adaptive leader, enabling them to guide their organizations through varied landscapes with confidence and precision.

Leading Through Disruption

Perhaps one of the most defining characteristics of adaptive leadership is the ability to thrive in times of disruption. Disruption comes in many forms—technological advancements, market shifts, political changes—and is often perceived as a threat to existing structures. However, adaptive leaders see disruption as an invitation to innovate, pivot, and excel. When faced with unexpected challenges, these leaders rise above reactionary responses, opting instead to analyze the disruption and adapt accordingly.

In a practical sense, leading through disruption requires a high degree of resilience and a readiness to pivot. Leaders must be prepared to reevaluate goals, reallocate resources, and, at times, abandon long-standing strategies in favor of new approaches. This often means asking difficult questions: What is no longer serving the organization? Where are the opportunities in this disruption? Adaptive leaders remain focused on these questions, using them as compass points to guide decisions and strategies amidst the chaos.

Resilience in leadership is not just a personal attribute; it is a quality that leaders instill in their organizations. By promoting a resilient culture, adaptive leaders create an environment where employees feel supported in the face of challenges. This resilience is fostered through transparent communication, psychological safety, and a commitment to continuous learning. Organizations that embrace this model are less likely to view disruption as a threat and more likely to engage it as a source of growth. Adaptive leaders build teams that not only cope with disruption but actively seek out the opportunities it brings.

The Power of Systems Thinking in Adaptive Leadership

A cornerstone of adaptive leadership is systems thinking—the ability to see beyond isolated issues and understand the interdependencies within complex networks. Adaptive leaders are skilled in zooming out to grasp the bigger picture, recognizing that actions taken in one area can ripple through an entire organization or even an industry. This broader perspective enables leaders to anticipate unintended consequences, a vital skill in a fast-paced world where even small missteps can have far-reaching implications.

Systems thinking encourages leaders to move beyond linear solutions. For example, a company experiencing high employee turnover might initially attribute the problem to poor hiring practices. However, an adaptive leader would delve deeper, considering factors like company culture, work-life balance, compensation, and growth opportunities, recognizing that these elements are interwoven. By addressing the root causes of systemic issues, adaptive leaders foster sustainable solutions that not only solve immediate problems but also enhance the overall health of the organization.

Applying systems thinking often requires a willingness to question assumptions and embrace complexity. Adaptive leaders refrain from overly simplistic solutions and instead embrace a mindset of curiosity, constantly asking, "What else might be influencing this situation?" In doing so, they cultivate an environment where innovation is not just a goal but a natural byproduct of a comprehensive understanding of the organization's ecosystem.

The Journey of Becoming an Adaptive Leader

The path to adaptive leadership is not a destination but a continuous journey, one that requires courage, resilience, and an unwavering commitment to growth. In a world where change is constant, adaptive leaders stand out by their willingness to evolve, to learn, and to embrace the unknown. They see themselves not as commanders but as facilitators, guiding their teams through a landscape of uncertainty with both humility and confidence.

This journey is both deeply personal and profoundly collaborative. Adaptive leaders strive to create inclusive environments where every voice has value, and where diverse perspectives are not only welcomed but essential to the decision-making process. They foster a culture of trust and accountability, encouraging others to take ownership of their work and to innovate without fear of failure.

In the chapters that follow, we will dive deeper into the tools, strategies, and mindsets that define adaptive leadership. From mastering resilience to honing decision-making in high-stakes environments, this book is designed to equip you with the knowledge and skills needed to thrive as an adaptive leader. Remember, adaptability is not merely a skill to be learned but a mindset to be embraced. The challenges of tomorrow cannot be met with the solutions of yesterday, and as we embark on this journey together, may you find inspiration and practical guidance to become the leader that today's world demands.

Welcome to the world of adaptive leadership, where the possibilities are as vast as the challenges are complex. The road ahead may be uncharted, but with the right mindset, you have the potential to not only navigate it but to lead others toward a future of resilience, innovation, and unparalleled success.

Reflective Challenges for Adaptive Leadership

1. How Open Are You to Transformative Change?

In adaptive leadership, embracing change isn't just about acceptance; it's about fostering an appetite for growth that goes beyond traditional boundaries. Reflecting on your relationship with change means probing deeper than the surface, where platitudes of resilience often reside. Leaders who genuinely adapt don't just react to change but actively pursue it, seeking ways to infuse their teams and organizations with the boldness to question existing norms and challenge the status quo. However, cultivating this kind of transformative openness requires internal alignment. This process isn't without its challenges—it demands honesty, self-awareness, and a willingness to confront discomfort.

Begin by reflecting on recent decisions in your role as a leader. Were there moments when you chose a comfortable, predictable route over a more innovative, yet uncertain, approach? Think about the reasoning behind these choices. Was there a reluctance to engage with ambiguity? Or perhaps an underlying fear of missteps in uncharted territory? It's natural to seek stable ground, but adaptive leaders understand that the path of least resistance often leads to stagnation. This challenge is an invitation to examine your decision-making patterns through a critical, open lens.

Consider journaling about an experience in which you faced significant resistance to change, either from within yourself or from your team. Analyze the emotions involved, the stakes, and the ultimate outcome. Did this experience reinforce your commitment to adaptive thinking, or did it highlight areas where improvement is needed? For adaptive leaders, each reflection offers a lesson. By consciously examining your experiences, you gain insight into your relationship with change and build the foundation to welcome it with confidence, making bold choices that align with a future-oriented vision.

Now, ask yourself: if you were to adopt a mindset where change is not just tolerated but actively sought, what possibilities might open up for you and your team? Adaptive leadership means framing change as a vital ingredient for success, not an obstacle. Use this challenge as a springboard to redefine your approach to transformation. Aim to become a catalyst for innovation, a leader who isn't afraid to step into uncertainty but embraces it as a cornerstone of growth. Over time, as you integrate this mindset, you'll find that your team, too, begins to view change not as a threat but as a powerful opportunity.

2. Are You Leading with Systems Thinking?

One of the core skills in adaptive leadership is the ability to view challenges through the lens of systems thinking. Instead of seeing issues as isolated events, systems thinking enables you to recognize the interconnected web of factors influencing any given outcome. But cultivating a systems-thinking approach requires an intentional shift from traditional, linear problem-solving to a holistic perspective that considers both short-term and long-term implications. Reflecting on how well you integrate this mindset into your leadership practice can reveal both strengths and areas for growth in your adaptability.

Begin by examining a recent decision you made that impacted various levels of your organization. Consider the broader repercussions of this decision. Did you account for how it would affect other departments, stakeholders, or long-term goals? Reflecting on this experience will provide clarity on your default approach to problem-solving. Were you able to anticipate unintended consequences, or did you find yourself surprised by outcomes you hadn't foreseen? Adaptive leaders cultivate a habit of considering how every decision is part of a larger ecosystem, where even small actions can have ripple effects.

To deepen your systems-thinking skills, practice looking beyond the immediate challenges of any situation and consider the broader organizational structure. For instance, if there's high turnover in a particular department, the tendency might be to focus solely on recruitment strategies. However, systems thinking would encourage you to dig deeper—what cultural factors might be contributing? Are there systemic issues related to leadership, team dynamics, or workload distribution that play a role? Adaptive leaders don't settle for surface solutions; they aim to address root causes, understanding that true change comes from aligning short-term fixes with long-term stability.

This challenge asks you to embrace complexity and to see it as a powerful resource rather than an obstacle. Consider how you can incorporate systems thinking into your daily leadership practice, from planning to communication, strategy to feedback. Developing this habit will empower you to make informed decisions that account for both immediate needs and the broader goals of your organization. Ultimately, systems thinking is a vital skill in adaptive leadership, equipping you to navigate intricate challenges with clarity and foresight, ensuring that your decisions build resilience and long-term success.

3. Are You Cultivating a Culture of Accountability and Innovation?

Adaptive leadership isn't a solitary endeavor—it thrives in an environment where accountability and innovation are deeply embedded in the organization's culture. This challenge invites you to explore how well you are fostering these qualities within your team. An adaptive leader is one who empowers others, creating a culture where employees feel confident taking risks, sharing insights, and pushing the boundaries of traditional solutions. At the same time, they nurture a sense of accountability that ensures actions align with organizational goals and values. Striking this balance is critical to fostering an environment where adaptability can flourish.

Consider how you handle mistakes and failures within your team. Are they seen as setbacks, or are they reframed as learning opportunities? Adaptive leaders recognize that true innovation often emerges from trial and error. When teams feel secure in the knowledge that they won't be penalized for failures, they're more likely to experiment and take calculated risks. Reflect on a recent situation where an error occurred—how did you respond, and what message did your response send to the team? Adaptive leadership calls for a growth mindset, one that views mistakes as valuable stepping stones to improvement.

Fostering accountability in an adaptive environment means ensuring that each team member understands their role in the broader vision of the organization. Accountability doesn't just happen; it requires intentional communication, clear expectations, and consistent follow-through. Reflect on how you convey organizational goals to your team. Do you actively involve them in goal-setting and problem-solving, or are objectives handed down with limited input? Adaptive leaders engage their teams, ensuring that each member feels both ownership of and responsibility for their contributions. This approach builds a robust sense of commitment, as employees see themselves not as cogs in a machine but as integral players in the organization's success.

Challenge yourself to assess your approach to nurturing both accountability and innovation. Consider introducing regular team retrospectives where successes and failures are openly discussed. Use these sessions to encourage honest feedback and collaborative problem-solving, strengthening the team's adaptive capacity. By fostering a culture that celebrates learning and accountability, you empower your team to respond to challenges with creativity and resilience, building an environment that not only adapts but thrives amidst change. Through this intentional cultivation of culture, you will see adaptive leadership take root, creating a foundation of trust, innovation, and shared responsibility that will propel your organization into a future of sustained growth.

Steve Jobs, Elon Musk, and other visionary leaders exhibit characteristics that are deeply aligned with the principles of adaptive leadership. Their approaches to leadership and innovation offer powerful examples of how adaptability can fuel transformative impact in fast-paced, complex environments. Here's a breakdown of some key adaptive leadership qualities they embody:

1. Visionary Thinking and Embracing Uncertainty

   - Steve Jobs was known for his ability to foresee trends and opportunities that others couldn't yet imagine. He didn't just adapt to the tech industry; he reinvented it by introducing groundbreaking products like the iPhone, iPod, and iPad. His vision went beyond the products themselves; he anticipated how technology could enhance human experiences, combining art, design, and functionality in ways that challenged existing paradigms.

   - Elon Musk also exemplifies this visionary adaptability. Rather than conforming to traditional business strategies, Musk explores sectors that others view as high-risk or nearly impossible, from electric cars with Tesla to space exploration with SpaceX. He dives headfirst into uncharted territories, setting ambitious goals that push industries forward and making bold bets on technology's potential to transform the future.

- Adaptive Leadership Quality: Both Jobs and Musk thrive in environments of high uncertainty, demonstrating that adaptive leaders aren't deterred by ambiguity. They actively seek it out, using uncertainty as a launching pad for innovation and disruption. This requires both a strong personal vision and a willingness to challenge norms—qualities that define adaptive leaders in the face of complex and rapidly evolving challenges.

2. Systemic Approach to Problem Solving

- Jobs was a master of systems thinking, understanding that the success of Apple products depended on an interconnected ecosystem. From software to hardware, every detail mattered to him, and he demanded seamless integration. His famous emphasis on "end-to-end control" meant that Apple products were designed, built, and marketed with a holistic vision in mind, creating a cohesive user experience that distinguished Apple from competitors.

- Musk also exemplifies systems thinking in his ventures. At Tesla, for example, Musk goes beyond just manufacturing electric vehicles; he envisions a future where sustainable energy is accessible and integral to daily life. Through Tesla's ecosystem of electric cars, solar energy products, and energy storage systems, Musk addresses multiple interconnected factors in his mission to accelerate the transition to renewable energy.

- Adaptive Leadership Quality: Both Jobs and Musk demonstrate an ability to look beyond isolated issues and instead see the broader systems at play. They approach innovation holistically, ensuring that each element within their respective ecosystems aligns with their larger vision. Adaptive leaders, like Jobs and Musk, avoid quick fixes and focus on long-term, systemic solutions, driving sustainable progress.

3. Fostering a Culture of Accountability and Innovation

- Jobs demanded excellence from his teams, setting high standards and instilling accountability at every level. While he was known for his exacting nature, this approach built a culture at Apple where employees pushed their creative and technical boundaries, committed to achieving something meaningful. He encouraged a balance of creativity and responsibility, cultivating an environment where accountability was directly linked to innovation and excellence.

- Musk, known for his bold deadlines and ambitious goals, also fosters a culture of accountability and experimentation. He encourages employees to push beyond perceived limits, often inspiring rapid innovation through clear accountability and high expectations. At SpaceX, failures are seen as essential learning experiences rather than setbacks, which has enabled rapid progress in reusable rocket technology. This approach ensures that risk-taking is backed by responsibility, where each team member's contributions matter significantly.

- Adaptive Leadership Quality: Both leaders understand that innovation thrives in environments where accountability is paired with creative freedom. Adaptive leaders like Jobs and Musk create spaces where employees feel both empowered to innovate and responsible for results, ensuring that bold ideas come to life through a disciplined approach to execution. They encourage learning from mistakes, emphasizing that accountability does not mean avoiding risk but instead involves committing to continuous improvement.

4. Resilience and Determination in the Face of Setbacks

- Jobs faced numerous challenges, from being ousted from Apple in the mid-1980s to seeing projects fail. However, he used these setbacks as opportunities for growth, launching companies like NeXT and Pixar before returning to Apple to lead one of the most remarkable corporate turnarounds in history. His resilience in the face of adversity and ability to reinvent himself are quintessential traits of an adaptive leader.

- Musk's resilience is equally legendary. Faced with near-bankruptcy multiple times, from the early struggles at Tesla to financial difficulties at SpaceX, Musk persisted, often investing his own money to keep these ventures afloat. His resilience demonstrates a high tolerance for risk and a deep commitment to his vision, qualities that have enabled him to lead these companies through turbulent periods to success.

- Adaptive Leadership Quality: Resilience is at the heart of adaptive leadership. Both Jobs and Musk show that setbacks are not roadblocks but are instead part of the journey. Adaptive leaders like them demonstrate an unwavering commitment to their vision, showing resilience in the face of failure and using setbacks as fuel for future success. They remain focused on their goals, adapting to challenges with determination and persistence.

5. Empowering Teams and Cultivating Talent

- Though Jobs was a perfectionist, he recognized the importance of surrounding himself with talented people who shared his vision. He built teams of highly skilled professionals and empowered them to produce their best work. By setting high standards, Jobs created an environment where exceptional talent thrived, ensuring that the people around him were as committed to excellence as he was.

- Musk's approach to team-building is similarly rooted in empowering highly capable individuals. He is known for assembling teams that combine exceptional technical skill with a willingness to embrace bold challenges. Musk has often emphasized hiring for attitude and adaptability over experience alone, valuing those who can learn and adapt quickly to the evolving demands of his ambitious projects.

- Adaptive Leadership Quality: Jobs and Musk illustrate that adaptive leadership involves cultivating a team that not only possesses technical expertise but also shares a commitment to continuous learning and growth. Adaptive leaders invest in their people, empowering them to stretch their capabilities, pursue bold ideas, and contribute meaningfully to a shared vision. They understand that building an adaptable organization requires adaptable individuals who are encouraged to think, innovate, and grow within a supportive framework.

6. Relentless Focus on Customer-Centric Innovation

- Jobs' famous approach to design was to start with the customer experience and work backward. His commitment to understanding and anticipating customer needs was evident in every Apple product. Jobs's laser focus on creating an exceptional, intuitive user experience drove Apple to prioritize design, simplicity, and functionality in ways that revolutionized the tech industry.

- Musk similarly prioritizes customer impact, particularly with Tesla, where he's focused on creating not just luxury electric cars but a sustainable transportation model that benefits society. His drive to make Tesla a leader in the electric vehicle industry is rooted in a commitment to the customer's future needs—affordable, accessible, and eco-friendly transportation.

- Adaptive Leadership Quality: Both leaders demonstrate a deep focus on customer-centric innovation, a cornerstone of adaptive leadership. Jobs and Musk understand that in a fast-paced world, remaining attuned to customer needs and expectations is essential. Adaptive leaders anticipate these needs, using them as a compass to guide strategic decisions and product development, ensuring that innovation is always relevant and impactful.

Together, Steve Jobs and Elon Musk exemplify the qualities that define adaptive leadership. Their vision, systems thinking, resilience, commitment to accountability, and customer-centric innovation make them standout examples of how adaptive leadership can drive transformative impact. Their stories serve as powerful reminders of the potential that lies within adaptive leaders who are willing to challenge conventions, push boundaries, and lead their teams toward a future of endless possibilities.

CHAPTER 2: READING THE TERRAIN: SENSING, INTERPRETING, AND RESPONDING IN REAL TIME

As a leader in today's volatile, fast-paced world, understanding the landscape around you is no longer just an advantage—it's a necessity. Imagine leading in an environment where change is constant, where every decision needs to be assessed not only for its impact but for its timeliness. This chapter explores how leaders can sharpen their skills in sensing, interpreting, and responding to evolving circumstances. We're diving into what it really means to have your finger on the pulse and, more importantly, how to act on that knowledge.

The Art of Sensing: It's All About Being Attuned

Adaptive leadership starts with an awareness of what's happening within and around your team, company, or even the broader industry. Think of sensing as your early warning system. It's about recognizing the small shifts and subtle changes in your environment before they become big, potentially disruptive issues.

1. Cultivating Sensory Awareness as a Leader

The first step in honing your senses as a leader is learning to actively listen—not just to words, but to tone, body language, and what's left unsaid. Many leaders are inclined to focus solely on the hard facts, but adaptive leadership requires a soft-skills approach. For example, have you ever sensed unease during a team meeting, even when no one voiced a complaint? Often, those moments are your cue to dive deeper and explore what's truly on your team's minds.

Actionable Tip: Develop a habit of regularly checking in with your team members informally. People tend to be more honest and open in casual settings. By keeping a pulse on their morale, motivations, and challenges, you gather valuable insights into the subtle shifts that could impact performance and cohesion down the line.

2. Keeping an Eye on External Trends

It's easy to get absorbed in the daily demands of running a team or company, but adaptive leaders know that understanding the external environment is crucial. Whether it's a competitor's unexpected move or a new regulatory change, trends and events in your industry or society at large can affect your organization. The trick is to tune into these cues without letting them overwhelm your focus.

Real-World Example: Picture this: You lead a mid-sized tech firm, and there's been a surge in companies offering remote work flexibility. Observing this shift early allowed you to pilot a remote work policy in your company, giving you a head start in retaining top talent. That's the power of recognizing external trends—not only to prevent reactive decision-making but to proactively seize opportunities.

Interpreting the Signs: Moving from Information to Insight

Once you're actively sensing your environment, the next step is interpreting the data. In today's world, leaders are inundated with information. From data analytics dashboards to financial reports and customer feedback, the challenge isn't about having enough data; it's about knowing what to make of it. So, how do adaptive leaders move from information to insight?

1. Pattern Recognition: Finding the Narrative

Our brains are wired to identify patterns, but adaptive leaders take this a step further by training themselves to discern meaningful narratives from the noise. Pattern recognition involves looking at data with a discerning eye, identifying recurring themes, and understanding their implications.

Storytelling as a Leadership Tool: Storytelling isn't just for marketing—effective leaders use storytelling to make sense of data and to communicate insights in a compelling way. When you present insights as stories, you make them more relatable, helping your team connect emotionally and intellectually with the strategy.

For instance, instead of bombarding your team with numbers on customer churn, consider sharing the story of one customer's experience and how it reflects a broader trend. This approach not only makes the issue tangible but also sparks empathy and motivation among your team to address it.

2. Avoiding the Trap of Overinterpretation

One common pitfall in interpreting data is seeing connections that aren't actually there. Adaptive leaders need to remain aware of confirmation bias—our tendency to favor information that confirms pre-existing beliefs. Balancing healthy skepticism with open-minded analysis can prevent costly misinterpretations.

Practice Cross-Checking: Whenever you notice a pattern, don't hesitate to validate it by cross-checking with multiple sources. In some cases, getting perspectives from team members or departments outside your own can provide a clearer picture and help you avoid drawing conclusions too quickly.

Responding Strategically: Acting with Purpose and Agility

In an adaptive leadership model, sensing and interpreting data mean little without effective response. Adaptive leaders aren't simply reactive; they make conscious, calculated moves that position their teams and organizations for long-term success. The secret lies in balancing quick decisions with strategic thoughtfulness.

1. Speed vs. Deliberation: Knowing When to Act

The ability to respond with agility is crucial, but moving too fast can backfire if you haven't fully understood the situation. Adaptive leaders are masters of knowing when to accelerate and when to hold back. Sometimes, the smartest decision is to wait for additional data or clarification rather than making a premature call.

Example: Take Elon Musk's approach with SpaceX. While known for his fast decision-making, he's also demonstrated the wisdom of waiting when necessary. Before initiating a major mission, he often conducts multiple tests and re-evaluates data, ensuring he's not simply moving quickly but moving intelligently. Adaptive leadership doesn't mean racing through decisions—it's about being aware of the timing that best serves your goals.

2. Making Decisions with Incomplete Information

No leader will have a complete picture 100% of the time. Adaptive leaders are comfortable with ambiguity and know how to weigh risks and benefits in situations of uncertainty. One of the best tools here is scenario planning.

Implementing Scenario Planning: Scenario planning doesn't mean predicting the future; it's about preparing for different possibilities. For instance, in project management, adaptive leaders will often create three plans: one for the best-case scenario, one for the worst, and one for the most likely outcome. By thinking through these options, you give yourself flexibility and clarity, even when new information comes to light unexpectedly.

Adaptive Leadership in Action: Real-World Case Studies

Case Study 1: Sensing Market Shifts Early – Netflix's Pivot to Streaming

Netflix started as a DVD rental company, but as the digital world began to expand, Reed Hastings, Netflix's CEO, noticed an industry shift toward online streaming. By acting on this subtle change before the trend was mainstream, Netflix transitioned from rentals to streaming and positioned itself as a leader in digital media. The key here was Hastings's willingness to sense and interpret early signs in the industry, then strategically respond before competitors had a chance to adapt.

Case Study 2: Interpreting Customer Needs – Starbucks and Customer Experience

In 2008, Starbucks was struggling, with plummeting stock prices and declining customer satisfaction. Howard Schultz returned as CEO, investing heavily in reinterpreting customer needs by focusing on the "Starbucks experience." Instead of solely analyzing customer complaints, Schultz visited stores and gathered insights from employees, interpreting the deeper narrative behind customer behavior. This shift brought Starbucks back from the brink, showcasing the power of adaptive leadership through insightful interpretation of data.

Adaptive Leadership Tools and Techniques

As you practice adaptive leadership, here are some tools and strategies to help you apply these principles to your organization:

1. Situational Analysis Matrix: Create a matrix where you can categorize different scenarios as urgent, important, both, or neither. This helps in prioritizing response efforts and focuses your resources on the issues that matter most.

2. Weekly Reflection Meetings: Host weekly team check-ins to discuss emerging trends, challenges, and new data. This simple practice creates a culture of sensing and interpreting, keeping everyone aligned and responsive.

3. Decision Journals: Maintain a decision journal, where you document significant decisions and their outcomes. This allows you to review and refine your decision-making process over time, learning from both successes and setbacks.

Embracing an Adaptive Leadership Mindset

Adaptive leadership is less about adhering to rigid structures and more about developing an agile, open mindset. Being adaptable means staying curious, being willing to challenge your assumptions, and encouraging diverse perspectives. When you lead with flexibility and foresight, you're able to guide your organization through any challenge, navigating uncertainty with confidence and purpose.

The principles discussed here—sensing, interpreting, and responding—are essential to thriving in a complex, ever-changing environment. Adaptive leadership is more than a skill; it's a mindset shift that, once mastered, empowers you and your team to excel in any situation. So, as you finish this chapter, ask yourself: What's the first step you'll take to become a more adaptive leader? Remember, the ability to adapt is not a talent—it's a commitment to constant learning and growth.

Statistics that Highlight the Need for Adaptive Leadership

Adaptive leadership isn't just a modern trend; it's a necessity driven by the realities of today's dynamic business landscape. Statistics reveal the urgency with which leaders must adapt to changing conditions, make swift yet strategic decisions, and cultivate a workforce ready to pivot when required. Here are several powerful data points that underscore why adaptive leadership is critical:

1. Rapidly Changing Market Conditions: According to a 2022 report by McKinsey & Company, 75% of executives state that the need for agile, responsive decision-making has increased in the last five years due to market volatility, digital disruption, and unpredictable economic conditions. Companies that can adapt to these shifts see a 50% higher likelihood of sustaining growth and customer satisfaction than those with more rigid structures. These insights show that decision-making speed is critical to staying relevant, and they stress the importance of developing leaders who can quickly interpret and act on market signals.

2. Employee Expectations and Retention: A Gallup survey found that 82% of employees are more likely to stay with a company that promotes adaptability and leadership that values feedback. In contrast, companies with less adaptable leadership suffer turnover rates 1.5 times higher than those that prioritize flexibility. Given that the cost of replacing an employee can reach up to twice their annual salary, fostering an adaptive leadership culture isn't just beneficial—it's financially crucial.

3. Innovation and Market Competition: Research from the Boston Consulting Group highlights that companies that adapt their strategies and models at least once per year are more likely to outperform competitors by 25% or more in revenue growth. This statistic underscores the importance of continual innovation, even if it means disrupting long-standing traditions within the company. Businesses that pivot based on new data or industry trends don't just survive—they thrive.

4. Resilience During Economic Downturns: In a study by Deloitte, companies that adapted quickly during the COVID-19 pandemic—whether by shifting to remote work, diversifying product offerings, or accelerating digital transformation—were 45% more likely to recover to pre-crisis levels within a year. Adaptive leadership was cited as a primary factor in their resilience, underscoring how agile decision-making is instrumental in navigating unexpected disruptions.

5. Customer-Centric Changes: Data from Salesforce shows that 73% of customers expect companies to understand and anticipate their needs, with a strong emphasis on swift, responsive customer service. Adaptive leaders who prioritize sensing customer expectations and interpreting feedback are better equipped to make proactive adjustments, enhancing customer loyalty. For organizations, this means that those who can "sense and respond" to customer needs quickly are positioned to retain and grow their client base, particularly in competitive sectors.

Case Study: Kodak's Failure and Fujifilm's Transformation—A Lesson in Adaptability

The story of Kodak and Fujifilm is a powerful case study of how adaptive leadership (or the lack thereof) can make or break a company. Both companies were giants in the photography industry and, as of the early 2000s, shared a near-monopoly on the global film market. However, while Fujifilm thrived through the digital age, Kodak struggled and ultimately declared bankruptcy in 2012. The difference? Fujifilm's commitment to adaptive leadership and agility, contrasted with Kodak's resistance to change.

Kodak's Downfall: The Price of Inflexibility

In the 1970s, Kodak held a dominant position in the photography market, controlling nearly 90% of film sales and enjoying the brand loyalty of millions. Kodak's leaders were known for their strategic thinking and rigorous approach to long-term planning. However, when digital photography began emerging as a viable alternative to film in the late 1990s, Kodak's leadership faced a critical choice: to adapt or remain rooted in their successful, yet ultimately outdated, model. Kodak chose the latter, despite evidence that consumers and photographers were beginning to favor digital formats. Rather than investing in digital technology, Kodak continued to bet on its core product—film.

What went wrong? Kodak's leadership failed to sense and interpret the trends that were reshaping the industry. Executives believed that digital photography would remain a niche, slow-growing market, while the demand for traditional film would sustain their profits for decades. By the time Kodak acknowledged the shift, it was too late; other companies had taken the lead, and consumers had moved on. When Kodak finally declared bankruptcy, it had lost much of its once-unshakable market share, and its workforce had been reduced by tens of thousands of jobs.

Fujifilm's Transformation: A Case Study in Adaptive Leadership

In contrast, Fujifilm recognized the shifting landscape and embraced adaptive leadership principles. Even as early as the 1980s, Fujifilm's leaders sensed that digital photography could disrupt the traditional film industry. Rather than resisting this change, they sought to diversify and build resilience. Fujifilm invested in research and development, exploring how its existing technology and expertise could be applied to other industries. Recognizing that they couldn't rely solely on film sales forever, Fujifilm's leadership made strategic moves to enter new markets.

One of Fujifilm's most remarkable pivots was its foray into healthcare. The company's expertise in chemicals and film manufacturing proved valuable in the medical imaging field, and Fujifilm quickly became a leader in diagnostic equipment and pharmaceuticals. Fujifilm also invested in cosmetics, applying their chemical expertise to create skincare products. These seemingly unrelated industries became significant revenue streams and positioned Fujifilm as a versatile, innovative company.

Fujifilm's leaders also worked to create an adaptable organizational culture, encouraging employees to bring fresh ideas and challenging traditional practices. By fostering a sense of adaptability across all levels of the company, Fujifilm cultivated a workforce that was ready to explore new paths, helping the company remain resilient through changing times.

Reflections: Why Did Fujifilm Succeed Where Kodak Failed?

Fujifilm's success, compared to Kodak's failure, highlights the critical importance of adaptive leadership:

1. Proactive Sensing and Responding: Fujifilm's leaders were tuned in to the trends in digital technology and proactively responded by diversifying the company's focus. In contrast, Kodak's leaders relied too heavily on past success and were reactive rather than proactive, making changes only after competitors had seized the advantage.

2. Encouraging Innovation and Risk-Taking: Fujifilm's leaders created a culture where employees were encouraged to innovate and explore new markets, even if they seemed unrelated to film. By contrast, Kodak's rigid organizational structure stifled innovation, and employees were reluctant to propose ideas that deviated from traditional products.

3. Adaptability as a Core Principle: Fujifilm's leaders prioritized adaptability, not only at the executive level but throughout the organization. This enabled them to respond to industry shifts and emerging customer needs more effectively than Kodak, whose leadership resisted significant change until it was too late.

Thought-Provoking Questions for Adaptive Leaders

To apply the lessons from these statistics and the Kodak-Fujifilm case study, here are thought-provoking questions for leaders who want to foster adaptability within their own organizations:

1. Are you actively sensing and responding to changes within your industry? It's easy to get caught up in day-to-day operations, but adaptive leaders regularly engage with emerging trends and patterns. Leaders should ask themselves: Am I aware of the subtle shifts in my industry, and am I preparing my organization to respond accordingly?

2. How can you diversify your organization's strengths and capabilities? As Fujifilm demonstrated, applying core competencies to new fields can be a successful adaptation strategy. Leaders might ask: What are our organization's existing strengths, and how can we leverage them in new or unexpected ways?

3. Is your organizational culture conducive to adaptability and innovation? Kodak's reluctance to embrace digital technology partly stemmed from a culture that discouraged risk-taking. Leaders should reflect on whether their teams feel empowered to propose new ideas, test unconventional solutions, and think creatively about the future.

4. Are you prepared to act even when all the data isn't available? Adaptive leadership often requires making decisions with incomplete information. Leaders should consider their tolerance for ambiguity and assess whether they are cultivating an environment that embraces calculated risks when necessary.

The Path Forward

The world is changing faster than ever, and leaders who fail to adapt risk being left behind. The statistics, case studies, and reflective questions in this chapter serve as both a warning and an inspiration. Adaptive leadership isn't just about making decisions on the fly; it's a disciplined approach that requires attunement to the environment, the ability to interpret signals accurately, and the courage to take action.

Leaders who embody these qualities don't just survive in a fast-paced world—they thrive. Fujifilm's resilience and Kodak's decline illustrate a fundamental truth: adaptability can be the difference between a company that reinvents itself and one that fades into irrelevance. In a world where change is the only constant, leaders who embrace adaptability are well-positioned to navigate uncertainty, inspire innovation, and guide their organizations toward a prosperous future.

Statistic	Description	Source
75% of executives	State the need for agile, responsive decision-making has increased significantly in recent years due to market volatility and digital disruption.	McKinsey & Company, 2022
50% higher growth probability	Companies with adaptive leaders experience 50% higher growth and customer satisfaction than those with rigid leadership styles.	McKinsey & Company, 2022
82% of employees	Are more likely to stay at companies with adaptive leadership and feedback-oriented cultures.	Gallup Survey
1.5x higher turnover rate	Organizations with less adaptive leadership face turnover rates 1.5 times higher than those that promote flexibility.	Gallup Survey
25% revenue growth advantage	Companies that adapt strategies yearly outperform competitors by 25% or more in revenue growth.	Boston Consulting Group
45% faster recovery	Adaptive companies recovered from crises like COVID-19 up to 45% faster than less adaptable counterparts.	Deloitte Study
73% of customers	Expect companies to quickly understand and anticipate their needs, making adaptive leadership essential in customer relations.	Salesforce

CHAPTER 3: MASTERING DECISION-MAKING IN UNCERTAIN TIMES

In the constantly evolving landscape of today's world, leaders face a unique set of challenges that previous generations could only imagine. The pace of change has intensified; technology advances faster than most organizations can keep up with, global markets shift unexpectedly, and what once worked well may no longer yield the same results. As a leader, you're not just asked to make decisions—you're expected to make the right decisions, often without a clear roadmap or full set of information. If you've ever felt the pressure of navigating these complexities, you're not alone.

Take a moment to consider the last major decision you made in a professional setting. Think about the factors that influenced you, the people involved, and, perhaps most importantly, the uncertainty surrounding it. Did you feel fully confident? Were there risks you worried might derail your plans? In this chapter, we'll dive into how to confront uncertainty head-on and refine your approach to decision-making in ways that foster confidence, resilience, and adaptability.

Understanding the Spectrum of Uncertainty

When we speak about uncertainty, it's easy to think of it as something to be managed, even minimized. However, adaptive leaders recognize that uncertainty is an inherent part of the process and, in some cases, a powerful tool for innovation. Rather than seeing uncertainty as an enemy, the key is to understand its spectrum—what we know, what we don't know, and what we don't even know we don't know.

Imagine you're steering a ship across uncharted waters. Some days, you may have clear skies and calm seas. On others, the horizon might be shrouded in fog, with hidden dangers beneath the surface. This is the reality of leadership: you are steering your team, your organization, and perhaps even your industry into the unknown. The first step in mastering decision-making under these conditions is to embrace the ambiguity and recognize that it holds potential. By seeing uncertainty not just as a risk but as an opportunity, you'll set yourself apart from those who may only view it as something to fear.

The Power of Adaptive Thinking

Adaptive thinking is the cornerstone of effective leadership in unpredictable environments. It's what allows leaders to shift strategies, pivot quickly, and experiment without being paralyzed by potential failure. Think of it like a muscle—the more you practice, the stronger it becomes. Adaptive thinking requires a willingness to question assumptions, re-evaluate plans, and explore options outside the conventional frameworks that have traditionally shaped your field.

If you're ready to step into this mindset, start by acknowledging your biases. We all have them, and they color every decision we make. Adaptive leaders, however, make it a point to identify and challenge these biases actively. The next time you're facing a tough decision, pause for a moment and ask yourself: Am I leaning into a particular solution because it feels comfortable or familiar? If the answer is yes, consider it an invitation to expand your perspective. True adaptive thinking involves seeking out diverse viewpoints, gathering information from unexpected sources, and remaining flexible even when a decision feels almost made.

Scenario: Making a High-Stakes Decision in Real Time

Let's put this into practice with a scenario. Picture this: you're the leader of a team that's been developing a product for months. The launch date is set for next week, but suddenly, a competitor releases a similar product with added features you hadn't anticipated. Your team is shaken, and you can feel the pressure mounting. Do you stick with the original plan, or do you delay the launch to add competitive features?

In moments like this, adaptive thinking can be your best ally. You might first ask yourself: What's the worst that could happen if we delay the launch? and What are the risks if we proceed as planned? By assessing the impact of each choice, weighing not only the immediate costs but also the long-term implications, you allow yourself room to adapt to the current climate. You might also reach out to team members for their input, gathering diverse perspectives to help you see potential blind spots. When you build this collaborative approach into your decision-making, you transform what could be a unilateral call into a team-driven solution, empowering those around you.

Building Confidence in Ambiguous Decisions

Decision-making in uncertain times can feel like standing on a ledge, wondering if the net will appear only after you take the leap. But part of being a strong leader is understanding that not every decision will be perfect—and that's okay. The goal here isn't to make flawless choices but to cultivate the resilience to adjust and move forward, regardless of the outcome.

One way to build confidence in your decisions is by setting clear criteria beforehand. Define what success looks like for you and your team, and develop metrics to measure progress. For example, if your goal is to expand into a new market, outline the specific benchmarks you'll use to gauge whether it's working. This framework gives you a reference point, even when the terrain is unfamiliar, and it helps ensure that your team understands the "why" behind each move.

Case Study 1: Expanding into New Markets

Imagine you're the CEO of a mid-sized tech company that has seen steady growth in a competitive market. Your product, a sophisticated project management platform, has a strong base in North America, and expansion seems like a natural next step. Recently, your team has identified a growing demand in South America, and it looks like a prime opportunity. However, expanding internationally involves high costs, regulatory compliance hurdles, and potentially risky cultural adjustments. Your investors are excited about the idea, but your finance team has flagged that cash flow will be tight for at least a year if you proceed.

Take a moment here and place yourself in this position. What's your gut instinct? Would you say yes to expansion and take the risk of thin liquidity, or would you hold off to strengthen your existing market base? Consider the following questions as you think through this decision:

1. What's the competitive landscape like in the new market? Have you assessed potential local competitors, their pricing models, and any unique cultural factors that influence how customers make purchase decisions? It's tempting to replicate your North American strategy, but adaptive leaders know that success in one region doesn't guarantee success elsewhere. Have you, for instance, evaluated the needs of South American customers? If they prioritize different features, is your product easily adaptable?

2. How can you protect your cash flow while expanding? Expansion can sometimes mean financial strain, but maybe there are creative ways to fund this growth. Could you form a partnership with a local distributor to offset some initial costs? Adaptive leaders think beyond the obvious financial solutions, considering alternatives that reduce risk. If you could secure funding or partnerships that allow gradual growth in South America, would that make expansion more feasible?

3. What impact will this have on your core team? Expansion is exciting, but the operational and cultural challenges can impact morale if not managed well. Leaders often think only of the strategic side, but adaptive decision-makers weigh the effects on every layer of their organization. Have you considered building a dedicated team for the new market so that the workload doesn't overwhelm your existing employees?

Case Study 2: Leading Through a Crisis with Product Recall

Next, imagine you're the founder of a health supplement company that has built a solid reputation over the past five years. Sales have grown rapidly due to the trust you've cultivated with your customers. However, one day, a supplier informs you that a batch of ingredients may be contaminated. Although no health issues have been reported, there's a possibility that the batch may pose a risk to consumers. A recall would be costly and damage your brand's image, but ignoring the issue could lead to severe consequences if it turns out to affect customers.

This scenario brings intense pressure, and the stakes are high. If you were in this position, how would you approach the decision?

1. Would you lean toward a recall? On one hand, recalling the product would show transparency and a commitment to consumer safety. But there's a chance that the issue isn't as severe as anticipated, in which case the recall might appear unnecessary and erode customer trust in your brand's reliability. Consider your core values here. Is your reputation rooted in transparency, or have you built a brand focused on premium quality and precision? A recall could reflect these values, but it could also damage the trust you've worked to build.

2. How will you communicate with your customers? In times of crisis, adaptive leaders know that clear, open communication is key. Think about how you would structure your message. Would you emphasize caution and transparency? Or, would you prioritize the effectiveness of past measures to reassure customers that this is an anomaly? The way you handle this moment can determine customer loyalty. Adaptive leadership means recognizing that honesty builds long-term trust—even when it feels uncomfortable.

3. How can you use this experience to improve? Every crisis contains a lesson. If you decide to recall, this could be an opportunity to strengthen your quality control measures or perhaps build stronger relationships with suppliers. In the long term, could a recall inspire you to refine your operational processes, enhancing your brand's reliability? Adaptive leaders seize moments like this to introduce proactive change, ensuring that future challenges are met with even greater resilience.

Case Study 3: Disruptive Innovation vs. Core Stability

Our final scenario is one that many business leaders face as their companies mature. Imagine you're the head of a successful company in the online education space, providing digital training programs for professional certifications. Business has been steady, and customer satisfaction is high. However, new trends in artificial intelligence (AI) are rapidly changing the landscape, and some competitors are incorporating AI to offer highly personalized learning experiences. These companies are gaining traction, and some of your team members have begun pushing for similar innovation in your programs.

This moment places you at a crossroads between maintaining the stability of your tried-and-true methods or risking significant resources to explore AI integration. What's your first reaction?

1. Do you embrace the trend? It's natural to feel pressure to keep up with disruptive technologies, but adaptive leaders consider more than just trends. If you were to jump into AI, would it align with your current brand promise, or could it dilute the hands-on expertise that makes your training unique? Reflect on whether AI would truly add value or if it's merely an enticing, short-term appeal. Sometimes, maintaining core stability can be more effective in the long term, even if it means temporarily setting aside flashy trends.

2. Could you take a hybrid approach? Adaptive leaders often pursue incremental, cautious innovation rather than diving head-first. Could you consider a smaller AI pilot project that targets a specific demographic within your market? Testing on a smaller scale would allow you to evaluate its benefits and risks without fully committing resources. By monitoring the results, you gain valuable data that will guide larger-scale decisions later on. Would this feel like a better way to explore AI integration?

3. What's your risk tolerance? Integrating AI requires substantial investment—not just financially but also in terms of time and resources for training and deployment. Adaptive leaders understand their organization's risk tolerance and decide accordingly. Are you willing to invest in research, even if it means slowing down your core business temporarily? Or does the stability and loyalty of your existing customers make innovation feel like an unnecessary risk?

Cultivating a Reflective Approach to Adaptive Decision-Making

As we've explored, each case scenario provides complex layers of decision-making. Real-world leadership often means weighing competing priorities, managing risk, and balancing ambition with practicality. So, what's the common thread that adaptive leaders follow?

1. They reflect consistently. Adaptive leaders are intentional about building time for reflection into their decision-making process. Before making a choice, they pause, revisit their core values, and consider the broader implications of each action. How often do you take time to assess your own decisions, and what they might mean for your organization's direction?

2. They rely on feedback loops. Gathering feedback—from customers, team members, or even industry experts—allows adaptive leaders to approach decisions with diverse perspectives. Take a moment to think about your own feedback mechanisms. Do you have reliable ways to gather unbiased input before big decisions, or do you tend to operate within a close circle of perspectives? Expanding your sources can give you the clarity needed to make better-informed decisions.

3. They embrace continuous learning. Markets evolve, technology shifts, and customer expectations change. Adaptive leaders are lifelong learners, always open to acquiring new knowledge that strengthens their choices. Could adopting a learning mindset help you stay agile and keep up with industry trends? Consider what areas of your expertise could benefit from regular updates, whether through industry news, seminars, or feedback from peers.

Applying Adaptive Leadership Daily

To close, remember that adaptive leadership isn't just a strategy for major decisions. It's a mindset, a daily commitment to growth, and a continual refinement of how you make choices. Whether you're expanding into new markets, handling a product crisis, or contemplating disruptive innovation, adaptive decision-making involves embracing the complexities of uncertainty, engaging with various perspectives, and consistently building trust within your organization.

Each decision, no matter how small, is a part of your leadership journey. As you move forward, stay connected to your core values and cultivate the adaptability to navigate any challenges that arise. Are you ready to test your approach? The path may not always be clear, but with an adaptive mindset, you're equipped to turn uncertainty into opportunity—and lead your team through uncharted territories with confidence.

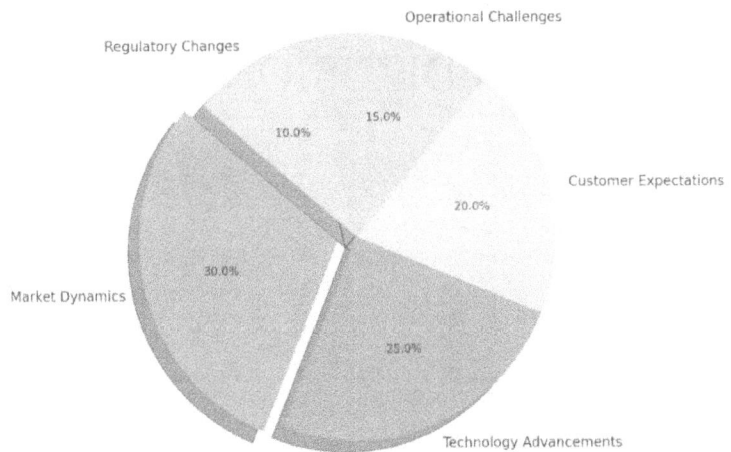

Key Factors Influencing Decision-Making in Leadership (2023)

CHAPTER 4: THE ADAPTIVE MINDSET IN DECISION-MAKING

SCENE: A QUIET CAFÉ IN PALO ALTO.

The reader is sitting at a wooden table near the back of the café. Across from them sit two legendary figures in tech: Elon Musk and Steve Jobs. The atmosphere is electric, brimming with the energy of big ideas waiting to be unleashed.

Reader: *"Thank you both for taking the time to discuss leadership and decision-making in such a fast-paced environment. It's a privilege to hear your perspectives firsthand."*

Steve Jobs: *leaning back and folding his arms, with a slight, confident smile* "The pleasure is ours. Talking about leadership today, especially adaptive leadership, is essential. We're in a world where innovation cycles are measured in weeks, not years. If you don't adapt, you're irrelevant."

Elon Musk: *nodding in agreement, his gaze intense* "Exactly. Adaptation isn't just some business buzzword. It's survival. With how technology advances, if you aren't keeping up, you're toast. You've got to be a futurist of sorts, constantly asking, 'What's next?'"

Reader: "What does that look like in practice, though? When you're leading a company that's trying to innovate at such a scale, how do you balance the present with this constant future focus?"

Steve Jobs: *pausing thoughtfully* "For me, it's about seeing the forest and the trees at the same time. In the early days at Apple, I couldn't just think about what we were building today—I had to think about the experience people didn't even know they wanted yet. Every product, every service, had to have a purpose. You have to dive deep into the consumer's mind and understand what they truly need, even if they can't articulate it."

Elon Musk: *chiming in, his voice brimming with excitement* "That's exactly it! People don't always know what they want until they see it. Like with Tesla, or SpaceX. With the Model S, it wasn't just about making an electric car. It was about showing that an electric car could outperform the best gasoline cars on the market. I wanted people to rethink what was possible. But here's the thing—while we're making something groundbreaking, we're also thinking about the next generation of cars and how to scale production."

Reader: "So, is there a specific mindset or set of principles you both follow in making these decisions?"

Steve Jobs: *gesturing with his hands, as if to emphasize each word* "I call it 'focused simplicity.' Every decision has to boil down to this one question: does this make the product better for the person using it? That doesn't mean the answer is always obvious, or even simple, but it does mean you strip away everything else. In a way, it's about doing less but doing it incredibly well. You can't just tack on features. You've got to subtract until you reach the essence of what really matters."

Elon Musk: *nodding thoughtfully* "I love that. For me, it's a little different, though. I tend to ask, 'Does this push the boundary of human progress?' Whether it's sending a rocket to Mars or designing the Cybertruck, there's this question of utility and vision. Does this decision help us achieve the mission, and can it scale to meet future demand? Every step has to lead toward a larger goal."

Reader: *leaning forward* "That's fascinating. So, it sounds like both of you value focus, but you also want to drive toward something greater—whether it's simplifying an experience or pushing humanity forward. How do you handle the pressure that comes with these decisions, especially knowing that not every innovation is going to work?"

Steve Jobs: *smiling, with a glint in his eye* "Ah, failure. That's something every great leader has to embrace. Failure isn't just a possibility; it's a necessity. Every failure teaches you something essential. At Apple, we had the Lisa computer—amazing technology, but it was a commercial disaster. That failure led to the Macintosh. The trick is to fail fast, learn, and move on. You don't cling to your mistakes. You mine them for gold and keep going."

Elon Musk: *with a chuckle* "You've got that right, Steve. Failure is just part of the process. At SpaceX, we had so many failed launches initially that people thought we were crazy. But every failure taught us something crucial. We iterated quickly, absorbed the lessons, and eventually, we nailed it. I tell my teams all the time, 'If you're not failing, you're not innovating.' It's about maintaining that mindset of resilience and pushing forward, even when things look bleak."

Reader: "So, how do you maintain that resilience, especially when the stakes are so high?"

Steve Jobs: *his tone softening, yet more intense* "I've always believed in doing what you love, something you're passionate about. When you're deeply committed to something, setbacks don't break you—they fuel you. I never saw myself as just creating products. I was creating experiences, almost an art form. And when you have that purpose, it gives you strength when times get tough."

Elon Musk: *looking thoughtful, a slight smile on his face* "For me, it's about the vision. I have a vision for humanity's future—a future where we're a multiplanetary species, where we rely on sustainable energy. That vision keeps me going, no matter how difficult things get. It's a North Star. I think adaptive leadership is about having a mission so compelling that it pulls you through the hardest moments."

Reader: *curious* "It sounds like both of you rely on something beyond just data or strategy—a kind of purpose. How do you stay aligned with that purpose, and how do you ensure your teams stay aligned as well?"

Steve Jobs: "It's about culture. At Apple, I worked hard to build a culture where people felt they were creating something meaningful. People want to feel connected to something larger than themselves, something that will make a difference. I think that's part of the secret—people aren't just driven by money or success. They're driven by purpose."

Elon Musk: *agreeing* "Culture is everything. At SpaceX, for example, we're tackling some of the hardest engineering problems known to man. If people didn't feel they were part of something historic, they wouldn't last a week. That's why we're so selective about who we bring in. People need to feel inspired, but they also need to be able to handle the intensity. Adaptive leadership isn't just about making fast decisions; it's about creating an ecosystem where people can thrive under pressure."

Reader: "That makes a lot of sense. It seems like adaptive leadership requires both flexibility and an unwavering sense of direction. How do you balance those two?"

Steve Jobs: *smiling* "Think of it as a jazz performance. You know the song, you have the structure, but you improvise along the way. You adapt, respond to what's happening in the moment, but you're always moving toward that final note. With each decision, you're refining, aligning, making sure you stay true to your vision, but you're open to the process being unpredictable."

Elon Musk: *with a laugh* "Or like a rocket launch. There's a mission, there are objectives, and a timeline. But you have to adapt in real time to what's happening around you. I think that's why we both talk about purpose so much. If you're clear on your mission, you can change your tactics and approach without losing sight of the goal."

Reader: "Thank you both so much for sharing these insights. It's incredible to see how much thought and purpose goes into each decision. One last question—what advice would you give to someone who wants to lead with the same adaptive mindset?"

Steve Jobs: *leaning forward, with that familiar intensity* "Stay curious. Question everything. Don't take shortcuts, and never settle. Keep pushing yourself to see beyond what's in front of you, to what's possible. True leaders don't chase after success—they chase after vision."

Elon Musk: *with a smile* "I'd say, dream big and be ready to go through hell to get there. If you want to make an impact, you'll have to adapt constantly, so get comfortable with the uncomfortable. Resilience and adaptability are your best allies. And remember, nothing worth achieving is easy."

In today's world, characterized by rapid advancements in technology and unprecedented access to information, leaders must operate with an "adaptive mindset" to remain relevant and drive innovation. Decision-making, once centered around consistency and predictable outcomes, now requires the ability to respond dynamically to changing circumstances, customer demands, and competitive pressures. This chapter delves into the adaptive mindset, examining key reflections from visionary leaders, practical challenges, and the essential skills needed for this form of leadership.

KEY REFLECTIONS ON THE ADAPTIVE MINDSET IN LEADERSHIP

1. Adaptation as a Core Competency

As Steve Jobs and Elon Musk emphasize, adaptability is not a supplementary skill—it is central to modern leadership. Jobs describes adaptive leadership as "seeing the forest and the trees" simultaneously. This metaphor suggests that leaders must maintain a dual focus: attending to immediate operational demands while staying attuned to emerging trends and the broader vision of their organization. Adaptability is about both anticipating change and responding swiftly. Leaders must continually ask, "What's next?" or risk becoming obsolete.

Musk takes this further, framing adaptation as an existential necessity: "Adaptation isn't just some business buzzword. It's survival." This underscores a reality in sectors like tech, where the pace of change can render even well-established organizations irrelevant if they fail to keep up. Whether advancing electric vehicle technology or venturing into space exploration, Musk views every challenge as a step toward broader goals. Each decision is rooted in adaptability, maintaining momentum even in an unpredictable environment.

2. BALANCING VISION WITH REAL-TIME FLEXIBILITY

Effective adaptive leadership also requires a balance between long-term vision and real-time flexibility. Jobs describes his approach as "focused simplicity," urging leaders to distill decisions down to their essential purpose. His principle of simplicity means eliminating distractions and focusing on what genuinely enhances the customer experience. This not only aligns decisions with purpose but also enables organizations to remain agile.

For Musk, this flexibility is about continuously pushing the boundaries of human progress. He advocates for an approach where every choice is evaluated against its potential to advance humanity. The emphasis here is on scalability—does a decision align with the company's mission, and can it support future growth? Both Jobs and Musk highlight that decisions must have both immediate utility and alignment with long-term goals.

3. EMBRACING FAILURE AS A GROWTH MECHANISM

Jobs and Musk both point out that adaptive leaders embrace failure as a critical part of the learning process. Jobs recounts the failure of Apple's Lisa computer—a project that, while unsuccessful, ultimately contributed to the groundbreaking Macintosh. Similarly, Musk emphasizes the learning value of SpaceX's early failed launches, each of which brought valuable insights, strengthening the company's path toward success. This acceptance of failure transforms it from a setback into a stepping stone, fostering resilience and instilling a culture of learning. The key, as Jobs points out, is to "fail fast, learn, and move on."

By fostering a mindset where failure is normalized, adaptive leaders create environments that encourage experimentation. Musk's saying, "If you're not failing, you're not innovating," reflects this philosophy. Risk-taking is integral to the adaptive mindset, where failure is not only expected but essential to moving forward.

4. BUILDING A PURPOSE-DRIVEN CULTURE

Jobs and Musk agree that a strong, purpose-driven culture is the foundation of adaptive leadership. Jobs focused on creating an environment where people felt they were contributing to something larger than themselves—a powerful motivator. Similarly, Musk notes that the difficult engineering challenges at SpaceX demand a workforce that is not only highly skilled but also deeply invested in the company's mission. By instilling a culture aligned with the broader vision, adaptive leaders can foster a sense of community and shared purpose that encourages resilience and innovation.

5. THE IMPORTANCE OF A NORTH STAR VISION

The conversation with Jobs and Musk highlights that an adaptive leader must have a guiding vision or "North Star." For Jobs, this vision was about creating meaningful, user-centric products, elevating technology to an art form. For Musk, it is a vision of a sustainable, multiplanetary future. This shared understanding of purpose allows leaders to inspire their teams and persist through challenges. When faced with setbacks, it is this vision that sustains resilience and keeps the organization moving forward.

PRACTICAL CHALLENGES IN ADAPTIVE LEADERSHIP

1. Balancing Short-Term Needs with Long-Term Goals

Adaptive leaders constantly face the tension between meeting current demands and investing in the future. A decision to focus on today's revenue-generating products may limit resources for R&D, constraining future innovation. Leaders must be willing to make trade-offs, knowing that too much focus on either the present or the future could harm the organization.

2. ENCOURAGING EXPERIMENTATION WITHOUT COMPROMISING QUALITY

Experimentation is essential to adaptability, but it can create operational inefficiencies or lead to inconsistencies. Musk's mantra of "failing fast" underscores the need for swift iteration. However, this rapid pace can strain resources and test an organization's tolerance for failure. Adaptive leaders must carefully manage this balance, fostering a culture of innovation while setting quality standards.

3. SUSTAINING TEAM ALIGNMENT UNDER HIGH PRESSURE

Keeping teams aligned with the mission is critical in high-stakes environments. As both Jobs and Musk point out, adaptive leadership requires a culture where employees feel connected to the vision. High pressure can challenge this alignment, potentially leading to burnout. Adaptive leaders must work proactively to maintain morale and ensure that employees remain engaged with the larger mission.

4. MANAGING INFORMATION OVERLOAD AND DECISION FATIGUE

The abundance of data and accelerated decision cycles can lead to information overload, potentially compromising the quality of decisions. Leaders must develop frameworks to quickly process information, identify relevant insights, and make effective decisions without becoming paralyzed by options. Jobs' principle of "focused simplicity" can serve as a guide—prioritizing clarity and relevance over volume.

DEVELOPING SKILLS FOR AN ADAPTIVE MINDSET

Skill	Description	Application in Decision-Making
Visionary Thinking	Ability to foresee industry trends and set long-term goals.	Helps leaders remain forward-looking while adapting to present needs.
Resilience	Embracing failure as a learning opportunity and persevering through challenges.	Allows leaders to recover quickly from setbacks and push forward.
Simplification	Stripping decisions down to their core elements for clarity.	Enhances decision efficiency and product focus, as Jobs practiced.
Risk Tolerance	Willingness to take calculated risks for potential innovation gains.	Supports a culture of experimentation, fostering rapid iteration.
Empathy	Understanding and anticipating user needs and market demands.	Guides customer-centric decision-making, crucial for product success.
Flexibility in Leadership	Balancing guidance with openness to new insights and approaches.	Ensures decisions can adapt without sacrificing strategic alignment.

STATISTICAL OVERVIEW: ADAPTATION IN MODERN BUSINESS

Statistic	Insight	Source
85% of CEOs report adaptation as crucial to business success	Highlights the growing emphasis on adaptability in corporate strategy	PwC CEO Survey 2022
45% of new product innovations fail within the first year	Underlines the risk of rapid innovation cycles and the need for resilience	Harvard Business Review
65% of employees prioritize purpose over salary	Demonstrates the importance of purpose-driven culture in retaining talent	Deloitte Millennial Survey 2023
Companies with adaptive cultures have 4x higher revenue growth	Correlates a flexible, innovative culture with business performance	McKinsey & Company

CHALLENGES AND REFLECTIONS FOR ADAPTIVE LEADERS

The adaptive mindset is integral for any leader navigating today's dynamic landscape. Jobs and Musk illustrate that it's not just about responding to change; it's about shaping it with purpose, resilience, and vision. The adaptive mindset involves a delicate balance between foresight and flexibility, clear focus and openness to failure. Leaders who cultivate these qualities are better equipped to foster innovation, drive meaningful change, and inspire teams through the unpredictable journey of modern business. Aspiring adaptive leaders are invited to reflect on their own approach: *How willing are you to embrace failure, focus on what matters, and build a culture where resilience and purpose lead the way?*

CHAPTER 5: NAVIGATING THE CONTROVERSIES AND CHALLENGES OF ADAPTIVE LEADERSHIP

In today's volatile global landscape, the concept of adaptive leadership has become both a beacon for transformation and a subject of intense debate. From its roots in the pioneering work of Ronald Heifetz and Marty Linsky, adaptive leadership has offered a strategic framework that goes beyond traditional top-down authority, encouraging leaders to tackle "adaptive challenges" — issues with no simple, pre-existing solutions (Heifetz & Linsky, 2002). However, the real-world application of adaptive leadership has spurred discussions on ethical dilemmas, inclusivity, accountability, and the limitations of adaptability itself. In this chapter, we delve into some of these controversies and outline the challenges future leaders must overcome to truly excel in adaptive leadership.

CONTROVERSY 1: THE PARADOX OF FLEXIBILITY AND STABILITY

Adaptive leadership thrives on flexibility, yet critics argue that too much adaptability can destabilize organizations. This tension was highlighted in a landmark study by the consulting firm McKinsey & Company, which found that while 90% of CEOs cited adaptability as a critical factor in success, 70% of them also expressed concern that over-adaptation leads to a lack of clear direction (McKinsey, 2019). For leaders, this paradox presents an ongoing dilemma: how to remain adaptable in a fast-paced world without sacrificing core values and stability.

Take, for example, the case of Nokia, whose leadership famously failed to adapt during the rise of smartphones. Nokia's rigid adherence to its existing model prevented it from embracing innovation swiftly enough, leading to a rapid decline (Vuori & Huy, 2016). In contrast, Apple's adaptive strategy, which blended responsiveness to consumer feedback with a steadfast commitment to its design philosophy, allowed it to seize market dominance. Yet even Apple has struggled to balance consumer demands with environmental sustainability, as critics point to the company's historical resistance to repairability to encourage regular upgrades.

CONTROVERSY 2: ETHICS IN ADAPTIVE LEADERSHIP

One of the most pressing controversies in adaptive leadership is its intersection with ethics. Critics argue that prioritizing adaptability can lead leaders down ethically questionable paths, particularly in high-stakes scenarios. The Wells Fargo scandal of 2016 is a stark example: executives fostered a hyper-adaptive culture focused on aggressive sales targets, which led to unethical practices, including the creation of unauthorized customer accounts. The short-term adaptability that allowed Wells Fargo to meet targets came at the expense of ethical standards, resulting in reputational damage and billions of dollars in fines (Brooks, 2017).

Research from Harvard Business Review shows that companies with strong ethical frameworks perform 5% better on average, underscoring the long-term value of ethical leadership (Gino & Pierce, 2019). For adaptive leaders, the challenge lies in balancing flexibility with an unwavering commitment to ethical principles, even when quick gains are possible through less scrupulous means.

FUTURE CHALLENGE 1: ADAPTING TO AI AND AUTOMATION

The rapid integration of AI and automation in business processes is reshaping leadership challenges. According to a 2021 report by PwC, up to 30% of jobs are expected to be at risk of automation by the mid-2030s, demanding that leaders not only adapt to technological shifts but also manage the social and economic repercussions of workforce displacement (PwC, 2021). Leaders like Sundar Pichai of Google and Satya Nadella of Microsoft have faced the challenge of leading adaptive change within organizations deeply entwined with AI development, balancing innovation with public accountability.

Adaptive leadership in this context requires a deep understanding of both technological advancements and the human impacts of these shifts. Nadella, for instance, has emphasized the importance of "empathy and empowerment" as Microsoft pioneers AI solutions while acknowledging ethical implications (Nadella, 2017). As AI advances, adaptive leaders will need to forge paths that maximize technology's benefits while safeguarding human values, data privacy, and ethical integrity.

FUTURE CHALLENGE 2: LEADING THROUGH ENVIRONMENTAL UNCERTAINTY

With climate change driving increasingly severe weather patterns and resource scarcity, environmental sustainability is no longer a secondary consideration but a central leadership challenge. Adaptive leaders in this realm are tasked with aligning business growth with sustainable practices, often without clear, immediate rewards. A 2022 Deloitte survey found that while 79% of executives agree sustainability is essential, only 40% have incorporated it into their business strategies effectively, reflecting the challenge of adaptive change in this space (Deloitte, 2022).

One notable example is Patagonia's former CEO, Rose Marcario, who transformed the outdoor apparel company into a model of adaptive leadership aligned with environmental sustainability. Marcario's focus on a mission-driven approach, including the decision to donate company tax savings to environmental groups, highlights how adaptive leaders can prioritize sustainable goals while maintaining profitability. The future demands adaptive leaders who can not only respond to immediate environmental challenges but also implement sustainable practices as a core tenet of their leadership strategy.

CONTROVERSY 3: THE INCLUSIVITY GAP IN ADAPTIVE LEADERSHIP

Adaptive leadership calls for inclusivity and collaboration, yet many organizations struggle to fully integrate diverse perspectives. A landmark study by the Boston Consulting Group found that companies with diverse leadership teams report 19% higher innovation revenue, showcasing the link between inclusivity and adaptability (BCG, 2018). However, the same report highlighted that only 10% of companies prioritize inclusivity in their adaptive leadership frameworks, suggesting a gap between theory and practice.

This discrepancy is often visible in tech companies, where adaptive leadership is essential for survival but inclusivity remains a significant issue. For example, while Facebook (now Meta) has been a leader in pioneering adaptive strategies, it has faced criticism for lack of diversity and the resulting limitations in addressing issues around content moderation and misinformation. Adaptive leaders of the future must bridge the inclusivity gap by creating environments where diverse perspectives are not just encouraged but actively shape decision-making.

FUTURE CHALLENGE 3: ADDRESSING MENTAL HEALTH IN FAST-PACED ENVIRONMENTS

As the pace of change accelerates, adaptive leaders increasingly face the challenge of maintaining mental well-being within their organizations. According to the World Health Organization, the global economy loses approximately $1 trillion annually due to depression and anxiety, which are exacerbated by high-stress work environments (WHO, 2020). Adaptive leaders must therefore prioritize mental health as a core aspect of organizational resilience, acknowledging that a healthy workforce is key to sustained adaptability.

Airbnb's CEO Brian Chesky is one example of a leader who has publicly advocated for mental health, recognizing its critical role in adaptive leadership. During the pandemic, Chesky implemented flexible policies and resources for employee well-being, allowing Airbnb to adapt to new market demands while supporting its workforce. Moving forward, adaptive leaders will need to create structures that promote mental well-being as foundational, not supplementary, to adaptive decision-making.

THE PATH FORWARD FOR ADAPTIVE LEADERS

As we look toward the future, adaptive leaders must navigate an increasingly complex array of challenges. From ethical considerations to environmental sustainability, inclusivity, and mental health, adaptive leadership is evolving to meet the demands of a fast-paced, interconnected world. To lead adaptively is to recognize that flexibility must be balanced with ethical, sustainable, and inclusive practices. Leaders who excel in this field will be those who continuously reassess, realign, and reimagine their strategies, combining innovation with a steadfast commitment to core human values.

The controversies and challenges explored in this chapter highlight both the potential and the pitfalls of adaptive leadership. As Heifetz (2002) reminds us, adaptive leadership is not about finding easy answers but about making difficult, value-driven choices in the face of uncertainty. For those willing to engage in the hard work of adaptation, the future holds not just challenges but profound opportunities to shape a more responsive, responsible, and resilient world.

In navigating the rapidly shifting sands of today's global environment, adaptive leaders are more crucial than ever. Yet this form of leadership, while flexible and responsive, is fraught with inherent challenges and ethical dilemmas. This chapter dives deeper into actionable strategies and future challenges for adaptive leaders, offering data-driven insights and practical advice. It also anticipates how adaptive leadership will evolve in response to increasingly complex demands from technological advancements, social accountability, and sustainability imperatives.

OVERVIEW OF KEY ADAPTIVE LEADERSHIP CHALLENGES: A DATA SNAPSHOT

Adaptive leadership is no longer a "nice-to-have" skill but a critical approach for any leader facing modern complexity. Below, we summarize key aspects of adaptive leadership using data from industry reports and academic studies.

Key Area	Challenge	Impact (%) or Cost ($)	Example
Technological Disruption	Balancing AI implementation with human job retention	Up to 30% of jobs risk automation by 2030 (PwC, 2021)	Google AI vs. Human Employment
Environmental Demands	Meeting climate goals while maintaining profitability	Sustainability focus adds ~15% in costs (Deloitte, 2022)	Patagonia's sustainable growth
Ethical Standards	Ensuring ethical decisions in fast-paced change	Ethics breaches can cause up to 50% stock drop (Forbes, 2020)	Wells Fargo's account scandal
Inclusivity	Fostering diversity in leadership	Companies with diversity earn ~19% more in revenue (BCG, 2018)	Meta's diversity challenges
Mental Health	Supporting employees in high-stress environments	$1 trillion lost annually to poor mental health (WHO, 2020)	Airbnb's wellness policies

These figures highlight how adaptive leaders must grapple with profound issues that impact both the workforce and organizational integrity. Addressing these challenges requires a proactive, ethically grounded approach. Below, we explore the implications of these areas in more depth and offer practical advice for navigating them effectively.

ADAPTIVE LEADERSHIP AND TECHNOLOGICAL DISRUPTION

Challenge Overview: The rise of AI and automation is transforming industries and redefining job structures. According to a 2021 PwC report, up to 30% of jobs globally could be at risk of automation by 2030. This reality demands that leaders not only adapt to emerging technologies but do so in a way that responsibly addresses the workforce's future.

ADVICE FOR LEADERS:

1. **Invest in Upskilling**: Rather than viewing automation as a means of reducing costs by cutting jobs, adaptive leaders should see it as an opportunity to enhance workforce skill sets. Organizations that invest 5% of their revenue in workforce development see up to 10% higher productivity rates, according to a Deloitte report (Deloitte, 2021).

2. **Implement Ethical AI**: Ensure that AI decisions are transparent and ethically grounded. In 2023, IBM introduced an AI ethics board to oversee decision-making processes, setting a precedent for accountability and consumer trust.

Future Considerations: As automation continues to advance, adaptive leaders will need to balance productivity gains with the potential social costs of displaced employees. Leaders who champion ethical AI and lifelong learning will not only stay competitive but also cultivate resilient, forward-thinking organizations.

SUSTAINABILITY: BALANCING PROFITABILITY WITH ENVIRONMENTAL RESPONSIBILITY

The need for sustainable practices has become essential for modern businesses. Research from Deloitte (2022) reveals that 79% of CEOs consider sustainability crucial, yet only 40% have effectively integrated it into their strategies. Adaptive leaders face the challenge of aligning growth with eco-conscious operations, requiring not just innovation but commitment to long-term environmental stewardship.

Environmental Leadership Model	Investment ($)	ROI (%)	Example
Carbon Neutrality	$5M initial cost	7% over 10 years	Microsoft's carbon-neutrality pledge
Circular Economy	$3M initial cost	10% over 5 years	IKEA's sustainable product lifecycle
Renewable Energy Shift	$10M initial cost	12% over 15 years	Google's 100% renewable energy commitment

ADVICE FOR LEADERS:

1. **Set Tangible Sustainability Goals**: Clear, measurable goals resonate more than vague promises. For instance, Microsoft pledged to be carbon negative by 2030, which involved an upfront investment but is projected to yield positive environmental and financial results.

2. **Encourage Transparent Reporting**: Consumers increasingly demand transparency. According to Nielsen, 73% of consumers are willing to pay more for sustainable products (Nielsen, 2020). Regular sustainability reports not only foster trust but also help leaders track progress and hold themselves accountable.

Future Considerations: As the effects of climate change intensify, adaptive leaders will need to innovate even more rigorously to reduce their environmental footprint. The future may see heightened regulations, making early adoption of sustainable practices not just ethical but essential for long-term survival.

THE INCLUSIVITY IMPERATIVE IN ADAPTIVE LEADERSHIP

Challenge Overview: Inclusivity has proven benefits for creativity and innovation, with companies boasting diverse leadership teams seeing 19% higher revenue from innovation (BCG, 2018). Yet many organizations struggle to incorporate inclusivity into their adaptive frameworks effectively.

ADVICE FOR LEADERS:

1. **Establish Diverse Decision-Making Teams**: Bringing diverse voices to leadership levels leads to richer, more comprehensive problem-solving. Research shows that inclusive teams make better decisions 87% of the time compared to homogeneous teams (Harvard Business Review, 2021).

2. **Implement Equity-Focused Policies**: Equality goes beyond hiring practices; it includes equitable promotion opportunities and fair wages. Salesforce, for example, conducts annual pay audits to ensure wage parity across genders and ethnicities.

Inclusivity Measure	Potential Impact (%)	Example
Leadership Diversity	19% innovation revenue	PepsiCo's diverse executive board
Equity-Focused Promotion Policies	20% higher retention	Salesforce's wage parity audits
Cross-Cultural Training Programs	15% increased creativity	IBM's global inclusion initiatives

Future Considerations: As globalization continues, adaptive leaders must be proactive in building inclusive teams that reflect diverse perspectives. This focus not only drives innovation but also prepares companies to better serve diverse markets worldwide.

MENTAL HEALTH: BUILDING RESILIENT, SUPPORTIVE WORKPLACES

Workplace mental health has emerged as a crucial adaptive leadership consideration, particularly in the wake of the COVID-19 pandemic. A WHO report (2020) indicated that poor mental health costs the global economy $1 trillion annually, underscoring the economic and human stakes.

ADVICE FOR LEADERS:

1. **Normalize Mental Health Conversations**: Adaptive leaders can foster psychological safety by openly discussing mental health, destigmatizing the topic, and ensuring employees feel comfortable seeking support. For example, Unilever introduced "mental health days" to encourage employees to prioritize their well-being.

2. **Provide Flexible Work Options**: Flexibility supports both mental health and productivity. The Future Forum Pulse Survey (2021) found that workers with flexible schedules reported 2x the productivity and 1.5x the job satisfaction of those with rigid hours.

Mental Health Initiative	Impact on Employee Well-Being (%)	Example
Flexible Work Schedules	2x productivity increase	Shopify's "Digital by Design" model
Mental Health Days	20% reduction in burnout	Unilever's mental health policies
Employee Assistance Programs	30% higher retention rate	Google's mental health resources

Future Considerations: As remote work becomes a mainstay, adaptive leaders will need to refine virtual support systems and invest in mental health programs that transcend physical office boundaries. A strong commitment to mental health can distinguish organizations in a competitive talent landscape, as younger generations increasingly prioritize well-being over traditional job perks.

THE FUTURE PATH FOR ADAPTIVE LEADERS: PRACTICAL TIPS AND TAKEAWAYS

Given the challenges discussed, future leaders must continually refine their adaptive skills. Below are actionable steps and key takeaways to help leaders build resilience and drive positive change.

1. **Embrace Continuous Learning**: Staying informed of industry trends is critical. Encourage ongoing education for yourself and your team through online courses, workshops, and industry conferences.

2. **Develop Transparent Metrics**: Quantifiable metrics for sustainability, inclusivity, and mental health progress help leaders make data-driven adjustments.

3. **Prioritize Ethics in All Decisions**: Implementing ethics boards, as IBM has done for AI, or conducting regular audits like Salesforce's pay equity checks builds a culture of accountability.

4. **Foster a Growth-Oriented Mindset**: Adaptive leaders are lifelong learners. Emphasize curiosity and experimentation over rigid planning, as this approach allows teams to adapt rapidly and effectively to change.

5. **Lead with Empathy**: An empathetic approach builds trust, reduces burnout, and promotes resilience. Adaptive leaders who prioritize empathy strengthen their teams and position themselves as supportive, progressive employers.

Adaptive leadership is a powerful, forward-looking approach essential for navigating a fast-paced, complex world. From the rapid evolution of AI to the increasing demand for inclusivity, sustainability, and mental health, adaptive leaders face formidable challenges. Yet within these challenges lie opportunities to redefine leadership, drive innovation, and foster lasting positive impacts. As leaders who balance flexibility with core values, ethics, and accountability, adaptive leaders can create not only stronger organizations but also a better world.

The future will favor those who can not only adapt but also inspire others to do so with integrity and purpose. By following the strategies and advice outlined in this chapter, readers are equipped with the foundational tools to lead adaptively in a world where change is the only constant.

APPENDICES

APPENDIX A: KEY CONCEPTS AND TERMINOLOGY IN ADAPTIVE LEADERSHIP

Term	Definition
Adaptive Challenge	Complex problems without easy solutions, requiring leaders to change mindsets and approaches.
Technical Problem	Issues with clear solutions based on existing knowledge, often solved by expertise or authority.
Holding Environment	A space—psychological, emotional, or physical—where people can tackle complex challenges.
Work Avoidance	Behaviors or tactics people use to avoid difficult changes or uncomfortable conversations.
Leadership vs. Authority	Leadership is the act of guiding change; authority is the power given by a formal role.

Source: Heifetz, R., & Linsky, M. (2002). *Leadership on the Line: Staying Alive through the Dangers of Leading*. Harvard Business Review Press.

APPENDIX B: PRACTICAL FRAMEWORKS FOR ADAPTIVE LEADERSHIP

1. **The Adaptive Leadership Framework** (Heifetz, Grashow, & Linsky, 2009):

   - **Observe**: Understand the full context, including technical and adaptive challenges.
   - **Interpret**: Identify patterns and key issues, avoiding assumptions.
   - **Intervene**: Make strategic interventions that disrupt unproductive patterns.

2. **Six Steps to Adaptive Change** (Cambridge Leadership Associates, 2010):

   - **Get on the Balcony**: Distance yourself from the chaos to see the bigger picture.
   - **Identify Adaptive Challenges**: Distinguish between technical and adaptive challenges.
   - **Regulate Distress**: Keep stress levels manageable while addressing the change.
   - **Maintain Disciplined Attention**: Keep the team focused on the adaptive work.
   - **Give the Work Back to the People**: Encourage team ownership of the solution.
   - **Protect Voices of Leadership from Below**: Encourage input from all levels within the organization.

Source: Heifetz, R., Grashow, A., & Linsky, M. (2009). *The Practice of Adaptive Leadership: Tools and Tactics for Changing Your Organization and the World*. Harvard Business Review Press.

APPENDIX C: STATISTICS AND DATA ON ADAPTIVE LEADERSHIP

Study/Report	Key Finding
McKinsey Global Survey on Change Management (2019)	70% of large-scale change efforts fail, primarily due to resistance and inadequate leadership.
Deloitte Insights on Workforce Development (2021)	84% of business leaders believe reskilling is essential, but only 10% have made significant progress.
BCG Diversity and Innovation Report (2018)	Companies with diverse leadership generate 19% more revenue from innovation.
WHO Global Report on Mental Health (2020)	Poor mental health costs the global economy $1 trillion annually in lost productivity.
PwC Workforce Disruption Report (2021)	Up to 30% of global jobs are at risk of automation by the early 2030s, requiring adaptive strategies.

APPENDIX D: REAL-WORLD CASE STUDIES IN ADAPTIVE LEADERSHIP

1. **Microsoft's Transition to Cloud Services**

    - **Challenge**: As the software landscape shifted to cloud computing, Microsoft needed to pivot from traditional software products to cloud services.

    - **Solution**: CEO Satya Nadella promoted a culture of "growth mindset," focusing on learning and adapting to change. Microsoft's Azure platform became a core revenue stream, demonstrating the success of adaptive leadership in embracing new business models.

    - **Source**: Nadella, S. (2017). *Hit Refresh: The Quest to Rediscover Microsoft's Soul and Imagine a Better Future for Everyone*. Harper Business.

2. **Patagonia's Sustainability-Driven Leadership**

    - **Challenge**: Balancing environmental responsibility with growth.

    - **Solution**: Former CEO Rose Marcario championed sustainability initiatives, including a commitment to using recycled materials. Patagonia's mission-driven approach increased customer loyalty and set an industry standard.

    - **Source**: Chouinard, Y., & Stanley, V. (2012). *The Responsible Company: What We've Learned from Patagonia's First 40 Years*. Patagonia Books.

APPENDIX E: FURTHER READING AND RESOURCES

1. **Books**

   - Heifetz, R., & Linsky, M. (2002). *Leadership on the Line: Staying Alive through the Dangers of Leading*. Harvard Business Review Press.

   - Heifetz, R., Grashow, A., & Linsky, M. (2009). *The Practice of Adaptive Leadership: Tools and Tactics for Changing Your Organization and the World*. Harvard Business Review Press.

   - Nadella, S. (2017). *Hit Refresh: The Quest to Rediscover Microsoft's Soul and Imagine a Better Future for Everyone*. Harper Business.

2. **Articles**

   - McKinsey & Company. (2019). *Leading with Purpose in Times of Change*. [Available online](#).

   - Gino, F., & Pierce, L. (2019). "Ethics and Innovation: How Companies Can Do Both." *Harvard Business Review*.

3. **Reports**

   - PwC. (2021). *Workforce of the Future: The Competing Forces Shaping 2030*. PwC Publications.

   - Deloitte. (2022). *2022 Global Human Capital Trends: The Social Enterprise at Work*. Deloitte Insights.

APPENDIX F: COMMON CHALLENGES IN ADAPTIVE LEADERSHIP AND SOLUTIONS

Challenge	Suggested Solution
Balancing Stability and Adaptability	Regularly assess and adapt core values and processes to current demands.
Managing Workforce Disruption	Implement upskilling programs and focus on continuous employee development.
Addressing Environmental Impact	Invest in sustainable practices and transparent reporting on sustainability goals.
Fostering Inclusivity	Build diverse teams and ensure equity in promotion and pay practices.
Supporting Mental Health	Offer flexible work schedules, mental health days, and accessible wellness resources.

Sources for Statistics:

- Heifetz, R., & Linsky, M. (2002). *Leadership on the Line: Staying Alive through the Dangers of Leading*. Harvard Business Review Press.

- PwC. (2021). *Workforce of the Future: The Competing Forces Shaping 2030*.

END

www.ingramcontent.com/pod-product-compliance
Lightning Source LLC
Chambersburg PA
CBHW070352230526
45471CB00006B/2536